SPACE OBJECTS

COMETS

by Elizabeth Andrews

Cody Koala
An Imprint of Pop!
popbooksonline.com

Hello! My name is Cody Koala

This book is filled with videos, puzzles, games, and more! Scan the QR codes* while you read, or visit the website below to make this book pop.

popbooksonline.com/comets

*Scanning QR codes requires a web-enabled smart device with a QR code reader app and a camera.

abdobooks.com

Published by Pop!, a division of ABDO, PO Box 398166, Minneapolis, Minnesota 55439.

Printed in the United States of America, North Mankato, Minnesota.

102024
012025

THIS BOOK CONTAINS RECYCLED MATERIALS

Cover Photo: Shutterstock Images
Interior Photos: Getty Images, NASA, Shutterstock Images
Editor: Grace Hansen
Series Designer: Victoria Bates

Library of Congress Control Number: 2024938592

Publisher's Cataloging-in-Publication Data

Names: Andrews, Elizabeth, author.
Title: Comets / by Elizabeth Andrews
Description: Minneapolis, Minnesota : Pop!, 2025 | Series: Space objects | Includes online resources and index
Identifiers: ISBN 9781098246969 (lib. bdg.) | ISBN 9781098247522 (ebook)
Subjects: LCSH: Outer space--Exploration--Juvenile literature. | Comets--Juvenile literature. | Solar system--Juvenile literature. | Astronomy--Juvenile literature. | Universe--Juvenile literature.
Classification: DDC 523.6--dc23

Table of Contents

Chapter 1

The Solar System

Our **solar system** was formed around 4.6 billion years ago. **Gravity** pulled together gas and dust to create the Sun. Space objects such as comets were formed from leftover gas and dust.

Our solar system is made up of the Sun, eight planets, and thousands of other smaller objects.

Watch a video here!

Comets are lumps of ice and rock that **orbit** the Sun. Some comets can be seen from Earth. They look like blobs with tails.

Comets visible from Earth come from the Kuiper Belt. But, most comets are too far away to see.

Chapter 2

Types of Comets

There are two kinds of comets. Short-period comets have an **orbit** of 200 years or less. They come from the Kuiper Belt and the **scattered disk**.

Learn more here!

Long-period comets take more than 200 years to complete orbit. They come

from the outer edges of our **solar system** in a region known as the Oort Cloud.

Chapter 3

Parts of a Comet

At the center of a comet is its nucleus. The nucleus is made up of ice, frozen gases, and rock. Nuclei can be anywhere between the size of a house to six miles (9.7km) across!

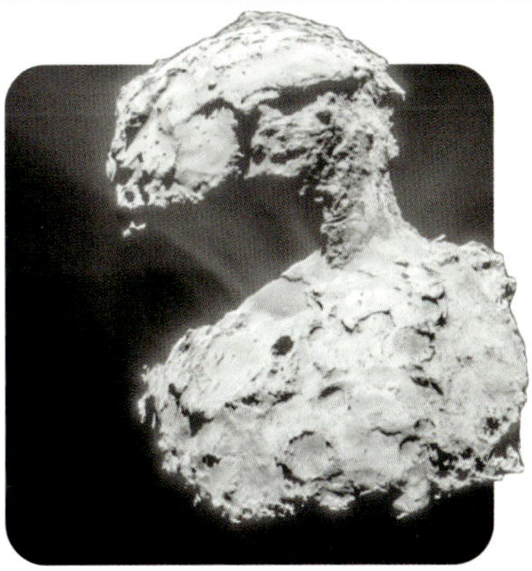

Explore links here!

PARTS OF A COMET

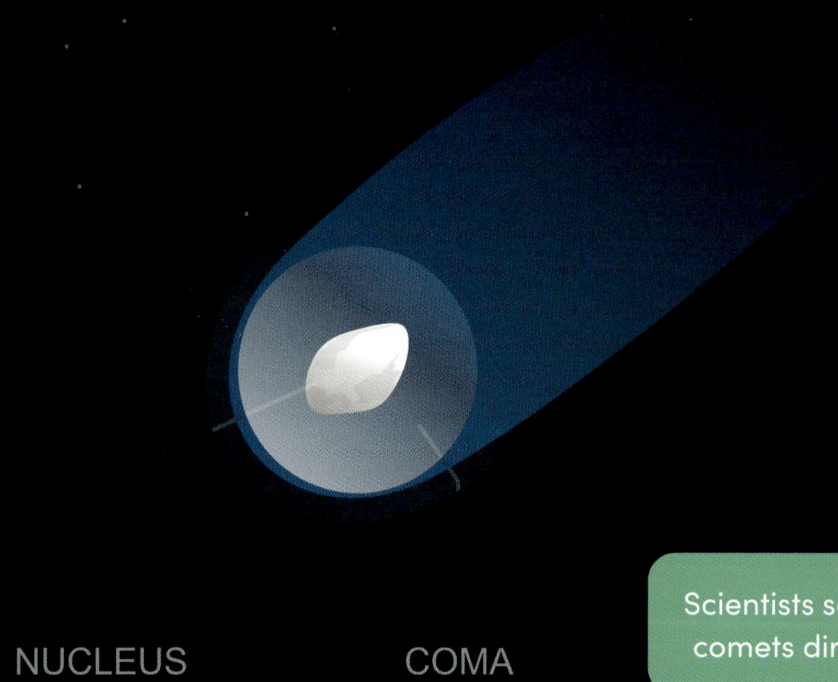

Scientists sometimes call comets dirty snowballs.

Comets' **orbits** go from the cold depths of space toward the Sun. As a comet gets close to the Sun, ice from the nucleus turns to gas. Pieces of rock turn to dust. The gas and dust form a cloud around the nucleus called a coma.

Solar winds push at the coma. Two tails appear. One tail is the dust from the coma. The other tail is the gas. Tails can be millions of miles long. They always point away from the Sun.

Chapter 4

Famous Comets

Halley's Comet is a short-period comet with an **orbit** of about 75 to 76 years. Halley's Comet can be seen from Earth. The next time it will be visible from Earth is in is 2061.

Complete an activity here!

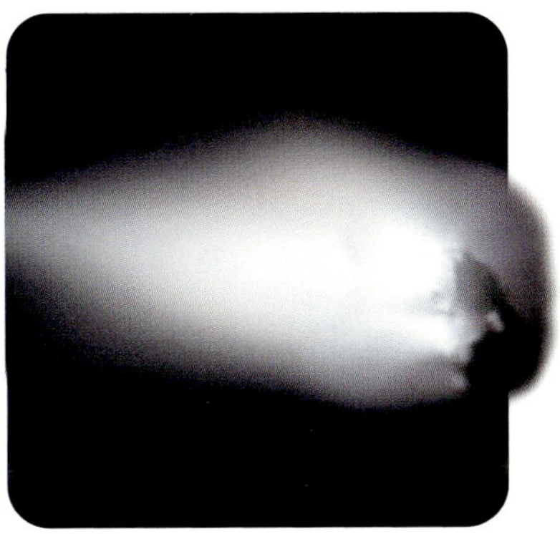

Hale-Bopp was discovered in 1995. Most comets have a nucleus that is a few miles wide. Hale-Bopp's nucleus is 25 miles (40km) wide! It is very bright. Humans could see Hale-Bopp without a telescope.

Making Connections

Text-to-Self

How old will you be the next time Halley's Comet returns to Earth's sky? Will you try to see the comet? Please explain your answer.

Text-to-Text

Have you read any other books about space objects? If so, how were those objects similar to or different from comets?

Text-to-World

Humans living long ago would have seen comets in the sky. Those humans did not have the technology to study comets. How do you think they may have explained bright moving space objects then?

Glossary

gravity – a force that pulls objects toward each other.

orbit – the path of a space object as it moves around another space object. To orbit is to follow this path.

scattered disk – a region in space that stretches far beyond the main part of the Kuiper Belt.

solar system – any system that includes a star and all of the matter which orbits that star, including planets and moons.

solar wind – the constant stream of charged particles given off from the sun.

Index

Online Resources

popbooksonline.com

Thanks for reading this Cody Koala book!

This book is filled with videos, puzzles, games, and more! Scan the QR codes* while you read, or visit the website below to make this book pop.

popbooksonline.com/comets

*Scanning QR codes requires a web-enabled smart device with a QR code reader app and a camera.